THE MINIATURE BOOK OF

ℬERRIES

CRESCENT BOOKS
New York

Published by Salamander Books Limited
129-137 York Way, London N7 9LG, United Kingdom

© Salamander Books Ltd., 1991

This 1991 edition published by Crescent Books, distributed by
Outlet Book Company, Inc., a Random House Company,
225 Park Avenue South, New York, New York 10003.

Printed and bound in Belgium

ISBN 0-517-06110-4

87654321

CREDITS

RECIPES BY: *Judy Bastyra, Mary Cadogan, Julia Canning,
Caroline Cowen, Kerenza Harries, Janice Murfitt, Cecilia Norman,
Lorna Rhodes, Sally Taylor and Mary Trewby*

PHOTOGRAPHY BY: *David Gill, Paul Grater, David Johnson,
Sue Jorgensen, and Alan Newnham*

DESIGN BY: *Tim Scott*

TYPESET BY: *The Old Mill*

COLOR SEPARATION BY: *P&W Graphics, Pte. Ltd.*

PRINTED IN BELGIUM BY: *Proost International Book Production,
Turnhout, Belgium*

CONTENTS

CHILLED FRUIT SOUP

6 oz red currants
6 oz black currants
6 oz cranberries
1½ cups medium-dry white wine
½ cup sugar
1 (2-inch) cinnamon stick
Finely grated peel and juice of 1 orange
1¼ cups water
1 tablespoon crème de cassis liqueur
⅔ cup dairy sour cream
Black currant leaves to decorate, if desired

*I*n a large saucepan, bring currants, cranberries, wine, sugar, cinnamon, orange peel and juice and water, to a boil. Lower heat, and cook gently until fruit is tender, about 15 minutes. Discard cinnamon stick. In a blender or food processor, puree fruit and liquid. Press through a nylon sieve to remove seeds. Cool, then refrigerate 1½ hours. Stir crème de cassis into soup, then pour into 4 to 6 chilled bowls. Carefully place a spoonful of sour cream on each serving, and, using a skewer, feather the sour cream attractively. Decorate with black currant leaves, if desired, and serve immediately. *Makes 4-6 servings.*

$\mathcal{S}$TRAWBERRY & AVOCADO SALAD

1 (1 pt) basket strawberries, hulled, sliced or halved
2 small avocados
Fresh mint leaves or strawberry leaves
HONEY LEMON DRESSING
2 tablespoons sunflower oil
2 teaspoons honey
2 tablespoons lemon juice
¼ teaspoon paprika
Salt and black pepper to taste

*F*or the dressing, in a bowl, stir together all the ingredients. Just before serving, pit, peel and dice avocado. Arrange with strawberries on 4 plates, drizzle with dressing and garnish with mint or strawberry leaves. *Makes 4 servings.*

NOTE: *A ripe avocado will give slightly when pressed lightly at the top or bottom. Very bruised, soft fruits are usually over-ripe. It is best to buy firm fruit and allow to ripen at room temperature.*

ℬERRY & WINE
SOUP

1½ lbs fresh or frozen mixed berries
(raspberries, red currants, black currants)
¼ cup sugar
1 cup sweet white wine
1 (4-inch) piece cinnamon stick
2 cups water
½ cup whipping cream, lightly whipped, to serve

*R*eserve a few good berries for garnish. In a large saucepan, mix remaining berries, sugar, wine, cinnamon and water. Place over low heat, stir with wooden spoon, until sugar dissolves. Simmer until berries are soft, 5 to 10 minutes. Discard cinnamon stick. Press mixture through a nylon sieve. Cover and refrigerate at least 1 hour. To serve, swirl cream into soup and garnish with reserved berries. *Makes 6 servings.*

CRAYFISH WITH STRAWBERRY DRESSING

1 cup dry white wine
2 cups water
1 carrot, chopped
1 small onion, chopped
1 celery stalk, chopped
1 leek, chopped
Bouquet garni
Salt and pepper to taste
2 lbs live crayfish
4 oz strawberries
2 tablespoons vegetable oil
3 tablespoons lemon juice
1 teaspoon coarse-grain mustard
Lettuce leaves (red lettuce, chicory) to serve

*I*n a large saucepan, place wine, water, carrot, onion, celery, leek, bouquet garni and salt and pepper. Bring to a boil, then simmer 5 minutes. Add crayfish, cover and cook until crayfish turn bright red, about 5 minutes. Drain and cool under cold running water. Reserve 4 whole crayfish. Carefully twist off the heads of the remainder, and peel away the tail shells. Arrange lettuce leaves on 4 plates; place crayfish on top. For the dressing, press strawberries through nylon sieve into a bowl. Stir in the remaining ingredients. Drizzle over salads. *Makes 4 servings.*

LIVER WITH RASPBERRIES

12 oz raspberries
2 tablespoons all-purpose flour
1 teaspoon dried leaf sage
Salt and pepper to taste
1 lb calves' liver, cut in thin strips
¼ cup butter
1 tablespoon finely chopped sage leaves
¼ cup raspberry vinegar
⅓ cup kirsch or framboise
2 teaspoons superfine sugar
Sage leaves to garnish

*R*eserve 12 raspberries for garnish. Press remainder through a nylon sieve; reserve. Mix flour with dried sage, salt and pepper. Put on plate or flat dish. Coat liver with the flour; shake off excess. In a skillet, melt butter, add liver and fry 2 minutes, turning to brown evenly. Add chopped sage and cook 1 minute. Using a slotted spoon, transfer liver to a warmed plate and keep warm. Skim excess fat from pan juices. Stir vinegar and kirsch or framboise into pan and cook 1 minute, stirring. Stir in raspberry puree, heat 1 minute then add sugar and check seasoning. Arrange liver on warmed plates, and spoon over raspberry sauce. Garnish with reserved raspberries, and sage leaves. *Makes 4 servings.*

TURKEY & CRANBERRY SALAD

Juice of 1 lime
½ cup dry vermouth
2 teaspoons honey
½ teaspoon dried leaf oregano
Salt and black pepper to taste
1 lb uncooked turkey breast slices, cut into thin strips
2 tablespoons virgin olive oil
1 small onion, chopped
1 cup fresh or frozen cranberries
Slivered peel of ½ orange
Orange slices and watercress sprigs to garnish

*I*n a bowl, mix together lime juice, vermouth, honey, oregano, salt and pepper. Stir in turkey, to coat. Cover, and let marinate in a cool place 2 hours. Lift turkey from marinade, letting excess drain off; reserve marinade. In a skillet, heat oil, add turkey and onion and cook, stirring occasionally, 5 minutes. Pour in reserved marinade. Add cranberries and orange peel and cook gently until cranberries begin to spit. Pour into a dish; cool. To serve, stir salad, then spoon into a serving dish. Garnish with orange slices and watercress sprigs. *Makes 3-4 servings.*

PORK WITH
JUNIPER SAUCE

1 (3-lb) boneless pork loin, skinned and trimmed
3 garlic cloves, slivered
Salt and pepper to taste
JUNIPER SAUCE
18 juniper berries, crushed
1 teaspoon green peppercorns, crushed
2 tablespoons brandy
2 tablespoons whipping cream
⅓ cup plain yogurt

*L*ay pork out flat, skinned side underneath. Cut several slits in pork. Insert garlic, season pork with salt and pepper, roll up and tie firmly with string. Season outside of pork, place in a roasting pan and surround with 2-inches water. Roast in an oven preheated to 375F (190C) until cooked, about 1½ hours. Lift from pan; cool.

For the sauce, pour off fat from cooking juices. Stir brandy, juniper berries and peppercorns into pan, bring to boil, reduce heat and simmer until reduced by half. Flame; cool.

Skim fat from sauce, then whisk in cream and yogurt. Check seasoning. Serve with cold pork. *Makes 6 servings.*

$\mathcal{V}$ENISON WITH BLUEBERRY SAUCE

6 (4-oz) venison steaks, well beaten
Grated peel and juice 2 oranges
Juice 1 lemon
3 tablespoons bourbon whiskey
½ cup olive oil
1 teaspoon dried rosemary leaves
1 teaspoon celery salt
3 bay leaves
Blueberries, bay leaves and orange slices, to garnish
1 cup light-brown sugar
1 tablespoon fresh lemon juice
⅔ cup water
8 oz fresh blueberries, rinsed, stems removed

*F*or the marinade, in a large shallow dish, mix orange peel, orange and lemon juices, whiskey, oil, rosemary and celery salt until well blended. Coat venison evenly, then refrigerate 6 to 8 hours, turning occasionally. For the sauce, in a small saucepan combine sugar, lemon juice and water. Heat gently, stirring, until sugar dissolves, then boil. Add blueberries, reduce heat and cook, stirring frequently, until thick. Cook venison under a preheated grill, 10 seconds per side, to seal. Brush with marinade. Cook until tender, about 5 to 7 minutes per side. Garnish and serve with sauce. *Makes 6 servings.*

*J*UNIPER
CROWN ROAST

3 tablespoons butter
1 small onion, finely chopped
½ cup hot well-seasoned beef stock
1 cup soft bread crumbs
2 tablespoons finely chopped dried apricots
8 juniper berries, finely ground
1 (2-lb) crown roast of lamb

*F*or the stuffing, in a medium-size saucepan, melt butter.
Add onion and cook until soft but not coloured. Remove
from heat. Stir in stock, bread crumbs, apricots and juniper
berries to make a soft but manageable mixture.

Generously oil a large circle of double thickness foil. Place
lamb in center, with bones pointing upwards. Press stuffing into
center. If using a covered barbecue, cook over medium coals to
desired doneness, about 30 minutes. If using an open barbecue,
tent joint with foil, and cook to desired doneness, about 50
minutes. Place a cutlet frill on each bone to serve, if desired.
Makes 4-5 servings.

CRANBERRY ORANGE STUFFING

2 cups cranberries
Grated peel and juice 2 oranges
3 tablespoons honey
2 tablespoons butter
2 onions, chopped
½ teaspoon ground black pepper
1 teaspoon ground mace
1 tablespoon plus 1 teaspoon chopped fresh sage
4¼ cups soft white bread crumbs
½ cup pine nuts
1 teaspoon salt
½ teaspoon ground black pepper

*I*n a saucepan, mix cranberries, orange peel and juice. Bring to a boil, cover and simmer very gently 1 minute. Off heat, stir in honey to dissolve, then pour into a bowl. In a saucepan, melt butter. Add onions and cook over low heat until soft. Stir in cayenne, mace and sage. Mix into cranberries with bread crumbs, pine nuts and salt and pepper. *Makes enough to fill an 8-lb turkey, or 2 duck.*

$\mathcal{B}$LUEBERRY MUFFINS

3 cups all-purpose flour
1 tablespoon baking powder
½ teaspoon salt
½ cup superfine sugar
2 eggs
⅔ cup milk
¼ cup corn oil
8 oz blueberries

*S*ift flour, baking powder and salt into a large bowl, stir in sugar and form a well in center. In a medium-sized bowl, beat eggs, milk and oil. Gradually pour into well dry ingredients, stirring to mix ingredients to smooth batter. Fold in blueberries then immediately spoon into a greased deep 12-cup muffin pan. Bake in oven preheated to 400F (200C) until well risen and set in center, about 20 to 25 minutes. Remove from oven and cool for several minutes in pan before turning out. Serve warm. *Makes 12 muffins.*

BERRY SOUFFLÉ

1¾ cups mixed red berries, thawed if frozen
½ cup superfine sugar
1 tablespoon strawberry liqueur or crème de cassis
5 egg whites
Powdered sugar to serve

*B*utter a 4-cup soufflé dish and sprinkle an even, thin coating superfine sugar around the inside. Place on baking sheet. In a food processor fitted with a metal blade, or a blender, process berries, sugar, and liqueur to a puree. Pour into a bowl. Whip egg whites until stiff peaks form. Using a metal spoon, fold 1 tablespoonful into puree, then pour puree into whipped whites. Lightly fold together until just evenly blended. Spoon into prepared dish. Bake in an oven preheated to 350F (175C) until risen and just set, about 25 to 30 minutes. Dust with powdered sugar and serve immediately. *Makes 6 servings.*

$\mathcal{W}$ILD STRAWBERRY
CHEESECAKE

1¼ cups finely crushed graham crackers
½ cup finely chopped hazelnuts
¼ cup plus 2 tablespoons butter, melted
3 eggs, separated
¼ cup superfine sugar
1½ cups cottage cheese
Finely grated peel and juice of 1 lemon
1 (¼-oz) envelope unflavored gelatin (1 tablespoon)
1¼ cups whipping cream, whipped
12 oz wild strawberries
3 tablespoons red currant jelly dissolved
in 2 teaspoons water

*I*n a bowl, stir together graham cracker crumbs and hazelnuts, then stir in melted butter. Press into a deep 8-inch springform pan; refrigerate until firm. In a bowl, beat egg yolks with sugar, cottage cheese and lemon peel. Dissolve gelatin in lemon juice; cool then stir into cheese mixture. Fold in cream. Whip egg whites to stiff peaks and fold into mixture with two thirds strawberries. Refrigerate until set. Spoon over cracker mixture. Garnish with remaining strawberries' and glaze with jelly. *Makes 6 servings.*

$\mathscr{K}$ISSEL

1½ (16-oz) cans black currants
½ (16-oz) can pitted dark sweet cherries
1 tablespoon arrowroot
Grated peel and juice of 1 orange
2 tablespoons crème de cassis
1¾ cups fresh raspberries
Mint leaves to decorate, if desired

*D*rain juice from fruits; reserve 2 cups juice. In a sauce pan, bring reserved juice to a boil. In a small bowl, blend arrowroot with orange juice then stir into juices in pan and simmer over medium heat, stirring, 1 to 2 minutes, until mixture is thickened. Stir in orange peel. Cool. Divide blackcurrants, cherries and raspberries between 6 individual serving dishes. Stir crème de cassis into sauce. Pour over fruit. Refrigerate. Decorate with mint leaves, if desired. *Makes 6 servings.*

CRANBERRY FOOL

12 oz package fresh cranberries
⅓ cup orange juice
¾ cup superfine sugar
1¼ cups whipping cream, whipped
Grated orange peel, additional fresh cranberries and fresh
leaves to decorate, if desired

*I*n a saucepan, mix cranberries, orange juice and sugar. Simmer until berries pop, about 10 minutes; cool. Using a wooden spoon, press through a nylon sieve. Using a metal spoon, fold into cream until just evenly mixed. Cover and refrigerate. Spoon into individual dessert dishes. Decorate with grated orange peel, cranberries and fresh leaves, if desired. *Makes 4 servings.*

SUMMER PUDDING

8 oz red currants
8 oz black currants
Juice of ½ orange
½ cup superfine sugar
1⅔ cups fresh raspberries
12 to 16 thin slices white bread, crusts removed
Red currants to garnish, if desired

*I*n a saucepan, combine currants, orange juice and sugar. Place over low heat, stirring occasionally with a wooden spoon, until currants are tender. Gently stir in raspberries; cool. Use 6 slices of bread to completely line 6 ramekin dishes; make sure there are no gaps. Cut circles to fit the tops of the dishes, from remaining bread. Strain fruit; reserve juice. Place fruit in dishes, pressing down well. Cover with bread circles. Spoon some of reserved juice over tops to soak bread well. Weight each pudding; refrigerate. Refrigerate remaining juice. To serve, turn puddings out onto individual plates and spoon juice over. Garnish with red currants, if desired. *Makes 6 servings.*

$\mathcal{S}$TRAWBERRY
YOGURT MOLD

1 (¼-oz) envelope unflavored gelatin (1 tablespoon)
3 tablespoons water
2 cups strawberry-flavored yogurt
1 pint strawberries

*I*n a small bowl, sprinkle gelatin over water; let soak until softened. Heat over a small saucepan of hot water, stirring, until dissolved. Remove from heat and cool slightly. Stir in a little yogurt, then gradually whisk into remaining yogurt. Pour into a wetted mold, or 4 wetted individual molds. Refrigerate to set. To serve, slice strawberries. Turn out mold, or molds onto serving plate, or plates, and surround with sliced strawberries. *Makes 4 servings.*

$\mathcal{B}$LUEBERRY WAFFLES

4 oz Petit Suisse cheese
2 tablespoons whipped cream
⅓ cup powdered sugar, sifted
1 cup blueberries
3 cups all-purpose flour
Pinch of salt
1 teaspoon baking soda
1 teaspoon baking powder
2 large eggs
1 cup milk
About ½ cup cold water
½ cup butter, melted

For the topping, in a small bowl, mix together cheese, cream and sugar; set aside.

For the batter, sift dry ingredients into bowl. Beat eggs and milk together. Gradually pour onto dry ingredients, stirring constantly, to make a thick, smooth batter. Add butter, and, if necessary, add water so mixture coats back of spoon. Brush both sides of heated waffle iron with oil. Fill one side with batter, close and cook until waffle is crisp and brown and steam no longer escapes. Remove waffle and keep warm. Repeat until all batter has been used. To serve, top each waffle with a spoonful of topping, and blueberries. *Makes 2-3 servings.*

*B*ERRY COMPÔTE

1 cup raspberries
1 cup loganberries
1 cup strawberries, halved
1 cup black currants
⅓ cup sugar
½ vanilla bean
1 tablespoon lemon juice
1 tablespoon water
Cookies to serve, if desired

*I*n a large saucepan, combine fruit, sugar, vanilla bean, lemon juice and water. Over very low heat, cook, gently stirring with a wooden spoon, until sugar dissolves. Cool. Discard vanilla bean. Pour into a glass serving bowl; cover and refrigerate. Serve with cookies, if desired. *Makes 4 servings.*